# BEYOND THE TETONS

*Poems From a Life Well-Wandered*

## LYNN SMITH

Copyright © 2025
LYNN SMITH
BEYOND THE TETONS
*Poems From a Life Well-Wandered*
All rights reserved.

No part of this publication may be reproduced, distributed, or transmitted in any form or by any means, including photocopying, recording, or other electronic or mechanical methods, without the prior written permission of the author, except in the case of brief quotations embodied in critical reviews and certain other non-commercial uses permitted by copyright law.

LYNN SMITH
For inquiries or permissions, contact:
lynnevansmith@hotmail.com

Printed Worldwide
First Printing 2025
First Edition 2025

ISBN: 979-8-218-85139-2

10 9 8 7 6 5 4 3 2 1

Interior Book Design by Walt's Book Design
www.waltsbookdesign.com

Cover design by Preston Smith

# BEYOND THE TETONS

# CONTENTS

FOREWORD .................................................................................................. 1
NATURE ........................................................................................................ 3
   *Old Dogs* ................................................................................................. 4
   *Benediction* ............................................................................................ 5
   *My Pet* ..................................................................................................... 6
   *Rattlesnake Bite* .................................................................................... 7
   *Elk Tracks* .............................................................................................. 8
   *A Gift* ...................................................................................................... 9
   *El Tigre* ................................................................................................. 10
   *An Ageless Challenge* ........................................................................ 11
   *Autumn Dance* .................................................................................... 12
   *Drifts of White* .................................................................................... 13
   *Footprints* ............................................................................................ 14
   *I felt the wind blow* ............................................................................. 16
   *The Web* ............................................................................................... 18
   *Arizona Is* ............................................................................................ 20
   *Cabin Fever* ......................................................................................... 21
   *Cottage 63* ............................................................................................ 22
   *Fire* ....................................................................................................... 23
   *If I met BigFoot* .................................................................................. 24
   *John Colter was here* .......................................................................... 25
   *Solanum Tuberosum* .......................................................................... 27
   *Steps of the Inca tail* ........................................................................... 29
HISTORY .................................................................................................... 30
   *Boots* ..................................................................................................... 31
   *Philadelphia* ........................................................................................ 32
   *On a Bench at Harvard Square* ......................................................... 34
   *Witness tree* ......................................................................................... 36
FAITH .......................................................................................................... 37
   *A Reflection* ........................................................................................ 38
   *Journal* ................................................................................................. 39

*God's Finger* ............................................................................... 40
*God's Finger* ............................................................................... 41
*Until Daylight Comes* .................................................................. 42
*Hope, Faith, Charity* ................................................................... 43
*Eternity Is* ................................................................................. 44
*Conflict* ..................................................................................... 45
*Winds of Change* ....................................................................... 47
*Beyond the Tomb* ...................................................................... 48
*Believers Prayer* ......................................................................... 49

FAMILY ........................................................................................ 50
*Child of Mine* ............................................................................ 51
*Flowers* ..................................................................................... 53
*Grandchildren* ........................................................................... 54
*LOVE* ....................................................................................... 55
*Maud Ann's Prayer* .................................................................... 56
*Memory of Their Love* ............................................................... 58
*Winter travel* ............................................................................. 60
*To Preston and Mindi* ................................................................ 61
*Teardrop* ................................................................................... 63
*The Cobbler* .............................................................................. 64
*The Yard Sale* ............................................................................ 66
*Rhythm sonnet #1* ..................................................................... 67

SELF ............................................................................................. 68
*Ancients* .................................................................................... 69
*BIRTHDAYS ARE....* ................................................................ 70
*Caged* ....................................................................................... 71
*Choice* ...................................................................................... 72
*Cow in the First Stall* ................................................................. 73
*Flame Within* ............................................................................ 75
*From the sea* .............................................................................. 76
*Inner Peace* ............................................................................... 77
*Layers* ....................................................................................... 79
*Wilted flower* ............................................................................ 80
*Windows* .................................................................................. 81

LIFE .............................................................................................. 82
*Laudanum* ................................................................................ 83

| | |
|---|---|
| Dependence – The Play | 84 |
| A Life Cycled | 85 |
| Echoes | 86 |
| Hatred | 87 |
| Joy | 88 |
| Life or Death | 89 |
| Life's Journey | 90 |
| Life's Smorgasbord | 91 |
| My Friend | 92 |
| Pattern | 93 |
| Staying Found | 94 |
| The Goal | 95 |
| Time | 96 |
| To Dream | 97 |
| Life Circled | 98 |
| Nights Sky | 99 |
| Written Words | 100 |
| Written word | 101 |
| The Painter | 102 |

# FOREWORD

They say that the beauty of William Wordsworth's poetry lies in emotion, the language of the common people of his time, and the natural world. He wrote poetry because prose was inadequate to convey the power of his feelings. So it is with Lynn Smith's poetry.

I never knew William Wordsworth. But I know Lynn Smith very well. Our lives have been intertwined for more than 40 years. From the beginning, we shared a deep love of family, wild places and wild things. He was new to Wyoming when we first met, both of us with young families and marooned in Cheyenne, Wyoming. Cheyenne has been described as "Des Moines with a rodeo" and we both felt more than a little out of place in our state's largest city, far from his mountains and my desert. We were strangers in a strange land.

But we grew to be brothers, maybe closer than brothers. Sandra supported him with love and patience through some thick and a lot of thin. The Smiths moved, but we stayed. They were in the Dominican Republic, then Idaho, then Wisconsin and then Arizona. But wherever they were, they took our hearts with them. We never lost touch. My brother was always my brother. And every time we are together, it's like we were never apart.

Over the decades, I have gained a firsthand appreciation for the depth of this kind and generous man. Even when his life was hard, his heart was soft. Even when hope was more than a little elusive, he held onto it with the iron grip born of hard work and honest love for God, family and the land.

Wordsworth said that poetry was a way to distill human experience and nurture growth in the reader. Lynn Smith offers the reader a warm hand up to a greater love and appreciation of the things that are truly important. God bless him for his work.

Walt Gasson

# NATURE

## Old Dogs

I love old dogs, their kind faces

Gray muzzles and wet tongues.

The way they lie their head in my lap.

Their eyes winning me over

Softly they peer into mine.

Penetrating my soul with endless love.

## Benediction

As shades of light crest the dark horizon

A coyote's howl penetrates the crisp air

Notes move over the mesa to the plain

The mournful call touches neighboring ears

Voices add to the melodious cry

A choir of performers sing their tale

Of sorrow, loneliness, famine and death

A benediction on the passing night

# My Pet

My pet Carl the snail

Carries his house on his tail.

I entered him in the snail race.

For weeks we practiced his pace.

He would race up one arm and down the other side.

Using the down arm as a slippery slide.

At the races where other snails, Matt, Bob, and Steve

Carl was faster than anyone could believe.

Across the finish he slid and slimed.

The victory was sublime.

# Rattlesnake Bite

I was bitten by a rattlesnake

Into his den I walked

I realized it was a mistake.

He warned me with his rattle

I thought there was room enough

Into his lair I toddled

He pumped his poison with a grin.

Leg swollen dying I thought

Who will call the next of kin?

# Elk Tracks

I see freshly placed elk tracks in mud.

I envision elk moving to pastures of green

I hear elk bugling in trees nearby

I dream of meadows, mountain peaks and clear streams

I cast a fly to hungry waiting trout

I long to see clear sky with bright stars above

Elks tracks have led me here

My dreams and yearnings to be realized

While sitting in a small cabin in Wyoming

# A Gift

Dew from Heaven

Caressing the earth

A gift, giving Life

# El Tigre

Volcano draped in green

Lying between conflict and war

People struggling for daily bread

Tourists search for handicrafts

Small boats lifeline to mainland

Shuttling people and supplies

Hunger, poverty, laughter

Dancing, singing, living in isolation

On an island draped in green

# An Ageless Challenge

A majestic antlered beast stands in an alpine meadow

Head cocked he bellows a shrill bugle into the frosty morning

Across the meadow a bugle of equal pitch vibrates the air

An ageless challenge given, now answered

two gigantic bull elk face in battle

Cows and calves quietly watch

Toned muscular bodies throw their weight into the fight

Dirt, sweat, blood, and hair form in a cloud around the dueling pair

One stumbles behind the force of his opponent

Immense pair of antlers plunge into his chest

Unable to continue he drifts away

A mature cow gives a few high pitched barks

The swelling herd moves around the victor

He extends his neck, roaring a victory call

Breathing short heavy breaths the defeated Bull stands alone

## Autumn Dance

Trees loaded in autumn colors awaiting release

Leaves vibrate shake and flutter with a gentle breeze they fall

They twist spin and float as the wind sets the rhythm and gravity the dance

Before settling to the ground awaiting a snow blanket for winter sleep.

## Drifts of White

Walking through snow covered wood

I spy a vixen wandering hungrily.

Thick orange fur hanging to a starving frame.

She moves through the snow.

With quiet grace and agility

Her black socking paws probing

Deftly she scours the sterile landscape.

On the bleached surface a shadow stirs

From a bush a rabbit emerges

Snowshoed feet propel it swiftly over the iced terrain

With speed and cunning the vixen bounces

The hare is no match against fangs.

A death scream penetrates the forest.

Drifts of white, now crimson

A world starving now satisfied.

## Footprints

Today I stroll along a woodland path

Scattered with footprints of my youth

Memories imprinted by time

Now exposed, they dance.

I recall sitting on a stream bank

Watching a family of otters slide and play.

A fish jumping to seize a fly from my line.

A great buck moves silently through aspens.

I visualize picking berries off loaded bushes

Into a waiting watery mouth

Eager taste buds explode

With a sweet-sour heavenly sensation

I witness kit fox playing at my feet

Gosling swim in front of my canoe

A cow moose nudges its calf

As it takes a first step into a marsh

Memories bright, colorful, translucent

Collide, merging past with present

Magnifying the simple truth

Footprints have neither beginning nor end.

# I felt the wind blow

It swirled dirt and sand

Drying the soil so nothing could grow

In the wind life seemed to fly away

I felt the sun, hot

Scorching, sweltering

Not one cold thing could be bought

All seemed to die under the sun's rays

I witnessed water flood the land

Destruction to all in its path

All earth was swept away by its demand

All living things seemed to drown

As I cried in despair

I saw a seed blown by the wind

It lit on a patch of ground just over there

Sand and dirt blown by the wind covered it just so

I beheld a rain drop dampening the ground

Sun warmed the soil

A plant of green peeked through the ground

Soon a flower grew bright

I looked to the heavens and understood

Wind, sun, and water

When wielded in God's hand mold and create

I prayed "God give me

The strength and patience

To be changed by thee

That I may become as the flower".

## The Web

One spring day I labored

My task's scope overwhelmingly loomed ahead

My presence seemed insignificant

I heard the giggle of a small boy nearby

Unaware of my labor he was observing a small bush

Laughing with delight intently he stared at a branch

Drawn from my work I stepped to his side

Peering at a single branch

I focused on a minuscule red spider

Completely unaware of its audience

It busily constructed its web

Precisely the intricate design was weaved

The web mosaic glistened as the red artist completed its masterpiece

For an unknown moment of time the boy and I were suspended

We applauded the simplicity of the complex mosaic before us

In the next instance the boy's mother called

After a brief pause, we parted

I returned to my labor now content to weave my own web

## Arizona Is

Sun scorched earth, skin piercing cacti, menacing snakes.

Deep rock canyons occasionally sprinkled with water.

Painted deserts filled with life and death.

Ancient volcanoes snow capped rising to the heavens

Riparian oases, and mountain islands dot the land.

God's showcase for all to see,

If one dares to venture out and stay awhile,

But do not forget to take water!

## Cabin Fever

Shut within a warm cabin I stare out into bitter cold

Walls of white driven by wind lap at the outer wall of my cell

Incarcerated; the howl of the blizzard

Calls me to test my strength against the tempest

As a caged beast freed, I burst through the door into the squall

Immediately encompassed by snow my essence merges with the storm

Freed I run, jump, crawl, and play becoming one with the turmoil surrounding me

Liberated I dance with the gale until its ferocity penetrates my flesh

Driven back into my cabin I swallow cups of hot liquid

As my frame thaws, now content I wait out the night

# Cottage 63

Stars brightly light an endless sky

Water rhythmically laps the rocky shore

A slight breeze moves through the blueberry bushes

The lonely call of a loon hangs in the wind

In the air are the notes of a forgotten tune

Clean air fills lungs as breathing slows

Troubles, cares, and worries drift away

To a destination unknown

# Fire

Sitting by a fire heat melts frost away

Crackling wood mellows unsettled spirits

Flames dance to the rhythm of burning logs

Each fiery tree reveals its natural life

One last event before ash returns home

A blaze painted of a rainbow, frolics

To captivated eyes keenly watching

Each splinter recanting its life story

The dying lumber gives a lasting gift

Changing a receptive heart forever

As fire cools vanishing flames flicker

A story of life now seared into the soul

To Uncle Fred

# If I met BigFoot

Would I run and hide?

Would I call the police?

Would I ask for his autograph?

Would we wrestle?

Would we compare foot sizes?

Would we sing a song in BigFoot language?

Or would I become his friend and explore his Big Foot world,

Learning about the plants and animals there,

Chasing butterflies and dancing a Big Foot dance,

Frolicking in the BigFoot Forest all day?

## John Colter was here

They found a stone in Sealer's field unearthed by plow and sweat

Upon it was etched John Colter was here, eighteen hundred and eight

All the inhabitants of my mountain home gathered to see the site

Experts from far and wide studied, concluding

Indeed, the great mountain man here had spent the night

To be like John Colter, free

Exploring wandering, living off the land

I, a boy of 13 years seemed to understand

With pack, knife, and gun set out to find John's trail

I discovered our souls were one

In a creek so clear, I saw my reflection with his

I took a bath in a beaver pond he had passed

Ate trout I caught like he would have with one cast

I felt the seductive lure of the Teton mountain range

John too had hiked over snow covered pass, peaks, and glaciers as I

Toiling in the heat of the desert sun I older now at the end of a day

Close my eyes and John Colter and I are again one

We hike, fish, and hunt all day in the mountains we hold dear

We watch as the sun sets on the Tetons

As we part, we promise to live life without fear.

## Solanum Tuberosum

Cut into a wedge and dropped into a hole.

Fertilized with smelly refuge.

Cultivated and watered with sweat and toil.

Days of warm sun and cool nights

Dug up a hill of starchy tubers.

Sorted, cured, and packed tight.

Potato, patato, tater or spud

Raw, fried, boiled, mashed, caked, or baked,

How can something so good come out of mud?

From Peru it traveled to distant shores.

In 1845 the potato crop turned to mush.

A million dead, families left Ireland by the score.

In France you have potato au gratin

England Fish and Chips, Scotland Shepard pie

Russia vodka from potatoes gone rotten.

For me, an Idaho Russet baked with butter and sour cream.

Elevates potato to a heavenly dish.

Fulfilling my wildest culinary dream.

## Steps of the Inca tail

Ascend skyward into the cloud forest

Hemmed in by carpeted vegetation

Carved from granite mountain cliffs

Wet and mossy upward they elevate


A ladder to the city of the Gods

Awaiting an adventurous spirit

To test fate scaling an orchid lined track

Risking plummeting off to depths below


Step by step sore muscles carry you

Leading along the heavenly staircase

To the mystic city of the Andes

Shrouded in clouds steps have lifted you here


To a city sculpted into mountain peaks

Awe and reverence envelop your soul

Caressed by the morning dew of heaven

Among llama at the top of the world

# HISTORY

## Boots

On Thermopylae's narrow mountain road

Against Persia's enslaved hoard

600 hardened Spartan feet

Freely make their final stand

Boots heaped high

Under Gettysburg's July sun

Soles worn thin by civil strife

Gray and blue stacked as one

A million pair of Europe's finest leather

At the Somme are thrown together

Burst to pieces by fire and lead

Now feed fields of poppies red

On Golgotha sandals,

Soaked by perspired blood

Witness;

God's great love.

# Philadelphia

Discussion, debate

Paper, quill

Discussion, debate

Hour is late

Paper, quill

No words to thrill

Discussion, debate

At stake a country's fate

Paper, quill

Document begins to gel

Discussion, debate

Texts now on slate

Paper, quill

A constitution to reveal


Discussion, debate

Paper, quill

The United States inaugurates

## On a Bench at Harvard Square

I sit on a bench at Harvard Square

In the air the past is sensed

Yet in the present I am

People hurry by unaware of time or space

A tall young woman purple from head-to-toe passes

Where students in uniform only once passed

A mixed-race couple kiss as they stroll by

They pass a school where only one race was admitted not long ago

Three blonde girls sip from Starbuck coffee cups

Next to a gate where men only once could enter

Bicycles, BMW's, taxis, and buses fly by

On roads where horses walked

I hear a protest for change nearby

Not far from where Revolutionaries were shot for protesting


I sit on a bench at Harvard Square

Where the present turns to the past and current – day becomes the future

## Witness tree

On cemetery ridge it stands

Leaves gently moving in the breeze

A witness to life on Pennsylvania land

Once young peppered by blue and gray lead

Leafless surrounded in blood-soaked soil

Heard a President honoring the dead

Observing hate, anger, and tears

Watching a country broken bleeding

Witnessing people healing throughout the years

Old wounded by war and time it lives still

Helping all to remember the pains of yesteryear

That the dreams of the fallen may be fulfilled

# FAITH

## A Reflection

I never see my face as others do

Only as bent rays of light from painted glass

A reflection with neither substance nor form

My facsimile without soul

Powerless to change a projected beam

I ponder my image, its depth and character

Dear maker of my soul

In whose similitude I am formed

Teach me to be content with my likeness

Give me patience for those who will not see

A desire to judge no one

The ability to serve all as equals

## Journal

The spirit touched my heart

I wrote my feelings with quill and pad

Closer to thee I felt apart


Time dimmed the spirit's light

I read my words long forgotten

Once again, the spirit was bright


Thank You father for what you have taught

# God's Finger

Lightening?

Frightening

Impulsive

God's Finger

Revealing our finite insignificance

Testifying his infinite power

# God's Finger

Lighting?

Frightening

Impulsive

Testifying his infinite power

Revealing our finite insignificance

# Until Daylight Comes

As the faraway sun sets to the west

Darkness blankets our present way of life

We scramble seeking sources of illumination

Darkness creeps into every corner of our world.

Without light we are enslaved by the night

Hope propels us to pursue brightness

There is faith in the impending sunrise

We sleep in the solace of the warmth to come

Sunrise brings the understanding that

There is no shadow that prevails over light

Our hope and faith now knowledge.

We will survive until daylight comes

## Hope, Faith, Charity

Hold on to hope

Strength of the heart

Believe in a better day


Faith never doubting

Apply sweat and toil

Leave the unseen to God


Charity, unrestricted love

Judge no one

Expecting nothing in return

# Eternity Is

Sun warm raising

Wounds healing

Light revealing

Brain remembering

Pain vanishing

Memories refreshed

Relationships deepened

Love strengthened

Forever and ever

# Conflict

Thick penetrating darkness surrounds me

Its weight sinks deep into my soul

Taking my breath away as I move from light

In the blackness I feel alone, isolated

Courage dissipates as despair encircles me

I ponder why light has left me

In the distance I see a small glow

I am compelled to ignore light

Yet as I gaze toward it, I have hope

Within darkness I am isolated

My mind teases," you are stronger in the shadows".

I'm torn between the comfort of darkness and the light of hope.

Eventually hope moves me toward light

Immediately I feel its warmth

In hope I endeavor to embrace light

I look forward to peace without darkness

I prosper in the serenity of light

I vow to shun darkness and embrace light

# Winds of Change

Winds of change dance in, out and through our lives

No one can escape or hide from its breath

Clouds of despair darken our path all will stumble

Each mixes their tears with its rain

The light of hope brightens our way inspiring all it touches

It quiets our fears and dries our tears

The fire of faith purifying burns a course straight and true

Directing us through life's journey

# Beyond the Tomb

Walking amongst granite with etched symbols

I spy names and dates of those I have loved

Green grass, brown dirt encases bodies of clay

Yet memories as an unending spring

Flow free renewing lives of yesteryear

They are before me smiling and dancing

I ponder, is there an unseen hand

Freeing souls to laugh beyond the cold tomb,

To walk and talk once again in peace?

Within my heart I know it to be true

We live on forever free of the grave

Again, united with family loved

## Believers Prayer

Beloved Father in heaven

Give me

        compassion to feel the pain of others.

        eyes to see that I might guide the blind.

        strength to lift those who cannot walk.

        a mind to understand the trials of the destitute.

        hands to learn the healer's art.

        feet to walk toward thee.

        knees that bend in prayer.

        a soul committed to carry out thy will.

Amen

# FAMILY

## Child of Mine

You came into my world with a rush of love and excitement.

Gazing into your eyes I knew we would be friends.

I had envisioned meeting you with great anticipation.

Our first night together was long and sleepless.

I vowed to teach you all you needed to know.

Quickly I learned, I was the one being taught.

You grasped to life at a speed I endeavored to understand.

I tried to have you run my race.

Time has schooled me.

You can run yours; I can run mine.

I have laid awake many nights thinking of you.

My heart has ached when you have struggled.

It has sung over your triumphs.

I know my life is better because of you.

Growing with you through happy and sad.

I have learned the meaning of Joy.

## Flowers

She walked as one that loves living.

In her step was the joy that comes with contentment

She gave of her soul all she received.

Asking nothing she blessed all she touched.

## Grandchildren

Lights given to help sight in twilight years.

Balls of fire reigniting youth in hearts.

Energy bars invigorating muscle.

Gifts bringing life to the aging soul.

Love its purest form.

# LOVE

Love originates in a twinkling

Magically caressing the heart

Enriching senses expanding hope

Aimlessness develops a purpose

A void is warmed overflowing

Life everlastingly transformed

Love cultivates deep adoration

Dedication seeding selflessness

Sacrifice unending witnessing

Friendship its purest form, eternal

Freely given continually

to you my cherished forevermore

# Maud Ann's Prayer

Life is hard we will learn

Spinning wheel spins through the night

All that is loved will return


Knitting mittens under lantern

Four sons she sent to join the fight

Life is hard we will learn


On bended knee she prayed with concern

Pleading her sons would be alright

All that is loved will return


Powers unite, Axis burns

Busy hands keep away fright

Life is hard we will learn


For dead sons' mothers yearn

She succors those who mourn their blight

All that is loved will return

Sister's son sent home in an urn

Serving, begging for God's requite

Life is hard we learn

All that is loved MUST return

# Memory of Their Love

After a day of battling regular life

I collapse into my soft chair

My deepened brow reveals the strain of the moment

As my heavy eyelids close, I envision them as they were

Laboring in a field dad's short legs and powerful torso are unmistakable

Running to him my legs tangle and I fall to the earth

In one quick motion he lifts me to his chest

Calloused hands and warm embrace wipe my tears and comfort my tender heart

In her apron mom is cooking bread

She spins around to meet me as I call

Cheerfully she hands me hot bread laden with butter and honey

Her food and soft voice sooth my young soul

Back in my soft chair furrows in my brow relax

Folding my arms, I feel a warm embrace

I can almost taste the butter and honey on my lips

I drift off to sleep consoled by the memory of their love

# Winter travel

Drifts of snow pile around our home

Firelight illuminates the cozy room

Mom in her rocking chair beckons us to travel a far

Opening her book, we are transferred away

Knights of Arabia, fairies dancing in the moonlight

Elves helping shoemakers, gold at rainbows end

Time is motionless a new chapter a different adventure

Shadows dancing on the wall each word becomes alive

Carried away in dreams soon eyelids close

Morning light finds us tucked in our beds tight

## To Preston and Mindi

Written 5:30 am March 27th, 2009

A new day comes

The light from the east

Chases away the night

Leaving yesterday behind

A day of change awaits

Life is renewed

Make the future today

Relish in the opportunities it brings

A day of hope lies ahead

Challenges of today will be conquered

Yesterday's mistakes forgotten

Tomorrows light will be brighter

A day of peace

Starting the day with prayer

Fears of yesterday are softened

Life eternal is opened


A day forever

Never again to taste loneliness

Sharing with those whom you love

Living today as your last

# Teardrop

I had not planned on it, yet a teardrop came.

A small amount of liquid in the corner of my eye.

I had believed it safe to think of you.

As the drop caressed my cheek thoughts continued regarding you.

Your laugh and smile encouraging me on

Our adventures and late-night talks.

One small bead now a torrent descending, washing away pain and loneliness.

Memories now cleansed, so pure and sweet.

I cannot help but smile, your life fashioned mine.

A simple teardrop has brought you back to me.

Once again, we can talk and laugh without pain.

Remembrance; strong and vibrant free to wash over my soul.

# The Cobbler

One well-seasoned Dutch oven

Two quarts of sweetened fruit

Three cups of cake or biscuit batter

Four tablespoons each, of butter and brown sugar

Five Coals under bottom, double on lid, cook til done


Scribbled on a frayed bit of paper

Used for years at hundreds of cook outs

Mother and father's cobbler sweetened the masses

Mom made the mix dad handled the Dutch oven

That combination created culinary magic


Vagueness of the recipe, deficient Dutch oven skills

Made duplation of their Cobbler challenging

Resulting in dozens of failures

I soon realized they were the missing ingredient

Skill can't be bought at a store

I can see them together cooking

Anticipating each other's needs

Enjoying working together

Smiling at the oohs and ah's

As crowds sample the cobbler

## The Yard Sale

Tables leaden with odds and ends of years past.
Items from eight decades of life and love
Quilts, saddles, magazines, books, an old broken sleigh
All marked, ready for sale.

The old woman continually carried treasures back into her home.
Confused, she leaves with her daughter before people arrive.
Backyard full of strangers looking for giveaways.
Items sold for pennies to make room for change.

Those with no recall buy memories.
A life of dreams walk away in moments.
Numerable coins mix with innumerable tears.
Tables and chairs were folded, doors locked.

The young family accept keys with a smile.
Content, the old woman eats alone in her new room.
Forgotten were the events of the day.
Over dinner her children cry.

I love you mom, Lynnie Evan 2008

# Rhythm sonnet #1

Then my heart functioned in precise rhythm.

Existing to feed the organ whole

Body, spirit, a soul without vision

Content with life passing on cruise control

Minute, hour, day, night, year, all tantamount

Desired no change, nor thought it likely

Transformation was too hard to surmount

Your entrance into my life was timely.

Witty, beautiful, kind, you caught my eye.

In one brief moment my heartbeat anew.

My reborn heart leaped, I cannot deny.

Altered afresh I knew you it was though

Daily toil an existence without strive.

Your sweet love now the rhythm of my life

# SELF

## Ancients

Before me is the world of the ancients

It calls to the deepest part of my soul

Troy, Athens, Constantinople, and Rome

Places of mystery and romance

Centers of learning and thought

Now only memories of greatness and glory

I am entering their world with hope

That their tears, fears, and glory

May instill a desire to reach my potential

## BIRTHDAYS ARE....

Like watching an old movie over and over Like bags of garbage

                                                                    thrown away once used

                    Hoping the ending will change never to be remembered

                                                                          But it never does

Like leftover casserole

When reheated again and again

It becomes stale and dry

                                                  Like bottles of new wine

                                                      With care and time

                                                 Grow better with age

Like smelling a fresh flower

Each time you smell it

Is sweeter than the first

                                                        Like a new car

                                                 When first bought

                                               Is clean and fresh

                                              Eager to be driven

# Caged

Surrounded by concealed iron bars

The lion lives a trapped existence

By day it paces the metal border

Nightly visions of freedom fill its head

For many reality is a cage

Trapped by camouflaged barriers of fear

Like the lion, we stride around our walls

Terror of action sealing confinement

Yet within each soul is given freedom

Reacting to our conditions with hope

Elevating the weighted bars of fright

Controlling life though choice and liberty

## Choice

Light in darkness

May grow or flicker out


Life touched by others

Changed forever, or cast aside


Water in a bowl

Washing clean or polluting


Choice a gift

Giving freedom or bondage

# Cow in the First Stall

The cow in the first stall was small and brown

She ate grain while she was milked

In the log barn behind my home

I first milked her sitting on a stool at the age of eight

She chewed her cud while I squeezed and tugged

After one hour, little milk, and sore hands

She kicked me indicating I was through

For the next ten years I was at her side day and night

Nature's nectar white and pure flew into the bucket

Sold for cash, it bought clothes and shoes

Consumed, it gave me vim and vigor

She taught me of work and patience

If I yanked she kicked the bucket

When I milked her late she got mastitis

If she had no straw for her bed she'd swat me with a dirty tail

While milking I dreamed of places afar

I composed and crooned great symphonies and ballads

We discussed my successes and failures

My future was planned while tugging her udder

After ten years I was ready to go on my own

Lessons taught at her side had been learned

As I loaded my car for college

My father loaded the cow in the first stall for market

# Flame Within

Within me lies a light small and dim

Yet it glows giving warmth

Flame is funny that way hidden, obscure

 Yet can beget another flame igniting innumerable fires

My ember seems so insignificant of no worth

Even a spark ignites flame only by sharing do I grow

# From the sea

The Sea calls me from deep within

From liquid I was born to land I am condemned

I need to be cleansed by rain

Bathed and softened, clay and dirt removed

Wash me tides of the sea purge my soul

Soak my skin and restore my frame

Stay near me clearwater that I might be renewed

Until my bag of bones is laid in soil and my soul freed

## Inner Peace

Have you ever craved silence?

The kind seldom felt

All around is quiet

You are left to yourself

Have you stood in stillness

Trapped in that instant

Each movement of your heart is heard

You are aware of your place in the world

I have experienced pure silence

In my youth I walked in winter wood

Large flakes of snow danced to the ground

I stopped in the trees and snow

I heard silence as it surrounded me

My ears searched only to find my beating heart

Solitude penetrated my soul

I perceived I was a small part of a greater whole

I stirred in time

A deer jumped from its bed

My silence broken

I hiked on anew

## Layers

Mom insisted on layers to keep us warm and safe

Sown, knitted, or tied, each layer was tucked just so

Gloves, socks, coats, and hat, shielding us from harm

At night, layers of quilts carefully placed keeping us from cold

I've lived my life with layers, meant to protect and guard

Each one tightly sown or woven, not to expose what lies beneath

As the butterfly must escape its cocoon

My metamorphosis relies on shedding layers

Once shielding, now holding captive

Only then can I, like the butterfly

Exposed, catch the wind in my wings, lifting.

# Wilted flower

A single arranged flower aged past prime

Rests in the appointed position

Appearance displaying effect of time

The remembrance of beauty touches me

I become encircled by its fragrance

The blossom engraved in my memory

The solitary floret changing my heart

Revealing elegance is enduring

To the unlocked soul it will be apart

## Windows

There are moments in life and time.

Small cracks through windows of our consciousness

Where if you are quiet and focus

You can peer through fissures to your soul.

There you glimpse who you are.

Who you may become.

The moments are fleeting, gone in an instant.

But if you grasp on to that tick in time

You are given a gift that changes your heart.

Motivating you to aspire to greatness

Transforming to a potential beyond yourself

Controlled by your action but given from God.

# LIFE

# Laudanum

**(POISON!)**

A cure for ailments

No pain or discomfort

A few drops, pleasing dreams

Where's Alice's rabbit

Pit in a pendulum

Shadow of Frankenstein

Stench of opium dens

Nightmare's play-acted

Independence consumed

Godsend or affliction

Pleasure or suffering

History's selection

## Dependence – The Play

Acted over and over demanding an audience.

Screaming for another performance

Applause louder but never enough.

Needing a ticket to attend; cost excessive.

Selling a soul one act at a time

Next performance never better than the first.

An ordeal enslaved by passion and desire.

Continually needing the next curtain call

Life passes, a delusional nightmare.

## A Life Cycled

Life is like water

Running, flowing, ever changing

At times rapidly passing by

Touching all, absorbed, rearranged

Cool still in a puddle

Warmed by sun and time

Reaches a seed buried, forgotten

Now changed forever becomes a flower sublime

Sea's pounding, tearing, ripping

Rivers running to the ocean

Sheets of rain drops fill cups

When touched by lips become a tear brought on my emotion

Ice, steam, mist, snow

A world never the same

Forests of green give oxygen

Water cycled touches all forever, reclaimed

# Echoes

In thought I smell a rose so sweet and rich

It moves my heart to remember my first kiss

I bite a ripe mango my taste buds exploding

My body beginning to move to an island beat of years past

I touch a fresh mowed lawn, fingers stained green

My hand raises quickly as if to catch a ball from a long ago played game

I hear the squeal of delight of a small child

Remembering my children's birth, tears of joy run down my cheek

I witness a sunrise so pure it warms me from head to toe

My knees bending thanking God for life

With only the echo of my once beating heart to break the silence

My soul is left to treasure simple joys

# Hatred

Hate breeds anger

Rage hatches discontent

Pride shatters hearts

Life becomes irrelevant

# Joy

Sadness encounters gladness

Hardship dances with fulfillment

Frustration encages pleasure

Sorrow marries happiness

## Life or Death

I have examined bodies, lungs exhaling, heart pumping

Blood flowing, cells serving, brain alert, eyes seeing.

I have beheld deaths silent complete finality

Corpses motionless, decaying, searching for a spark.

I have experienced life's pleasures, eternal love,

Satisfaction of hard work, the exhilaration of a glorious sunset.

I have chosen to live each hour sharing the vibrancy found in each day

Grasping the thrill of each moment absorbing the truth found around me.

I have faith life extends beyond the cold unyielding grave

To a life enriched by relationships exalted to eternal joy.

# Life's Journey

My life's Journey is akin to a skipping stone

Released from an unseen hand

Flung straight and true, towards a shoal of water.

Like the stone I can flit

Across the surface creating ripples

Or quickly sink without a splash.

# Life's Smorgasbord

Piles of food stacked high

Waitresses serving ham, steak, bread, and jam

Plates loaded with more than can be eaten

Life is like a smorgasbord

Opportunity piled high ready to be served

We each decide what to take

Some will eat meat others dessert

There are those who choose little

To them it is given to be hungry

Few are those who take the right amount

Meat, salad and always a little desert

They will be full and content

## My Friend

Around me are friends

Like a herd of cattle in a corral

They are friends cuz there is no place to go.

We do not mind the company.

We eat from the same stall

drink from the same trough.

You, my friend, are different.

 You are around me by choice.

You feel my joys and sorrows.

You find no fault in me.

You help me see

There is life away from the herd.

# Pattern

I've stood on a mountain peak

Rain and snow falling around me

Asking God to send the sun

I have lived in a desert

No water, dry as a bone

On bent knees praying for rain

I've asked for diamonds and gold

Complained when I had to dig

In the ground to obtain them

Change is the pattern for life

It's how you frolic in rain

Walk in blistering sun

Or dig in earth that counts.

## Staying Found

On the path of life are twists and turns

Side roads and diversions tempt travelers

Foul weather impedes vision and course

It appears that all hope has vanished

With compass in hand on bended knee

Through darkened wood the track emerges

Though lost you have discovered the trail

Disoriented, now enlightened

The secret to life is staying found

## The Goal

In the distance lies the goal

Over the next hill, through stream

Masked by clouds of mist, it remains unseen

Dark is the night

Cold is the day

Long and narrow the road

Few are those who perceive the goal

Despite darkness, rain and mist

With hope and faith the few push on

The goal clearly imprinted

They traverse mountains of snow and ice

Swim rivers and seas, until victory is theirs

Does the victory lie in obtaining the goal?

Or in the struggle born along the way.

# Time

Continuously marches on, we are left to dance on its ripples.

Waltz, jitterbug, salsa, or swing each chooses their dance.

However, time chooses the length and rhythm of the music.

## To Dream

Sparked by yesterdays, ignited with hope.

Dreams are born into a world of bygones.

Yet nourished with promise they will flourish.

Surrounded by despair and misery.

The fire of faith lights a path freeing ideas.

Enabling visions of bright tomorrows.

Kindle your dream to burn with belief.

It will melt gloom and evaporate agony.

Bringing you contentment, happiness, and joy

## Life Circled

Life is like water rapidly passing by flowing ever changing

Stirring, absorbing, rearranging.

Cool still in a puddle warmed by the sun reaches a dormant seed

Now changed forever becomes a flower sublime

Rivers running to the sea pounding ripping taring

Sheets of rain drops fill cups when consumed becomes tears brought on by emotion

Ice, steam, mist, snow, transforming the world

Water cycled touches all, forever reclaimed

# Nights Sky

We live in a predictable world consumed by a beginning and end.

Space is occupied with perceived success and failure.

Where the masses attempt to imprison time

One's very existence is examined and questioned

I gaze into the night sky.

On my back with cool grass encircling me

Unbound by the restraints from this realm

I stare into the vastness of the cosmos

Though the darkness above points of light sparkle

Mapping out endless possibilities

Time itself freed to reveal the truth there is no start or finish

Reality penetrates my soul to, life, time, and space unending.

## Written Words

Lines: short, fat, and tall

Red, black, blue and green

Drawn, stamped, etched or sprayed.

Thought: happy, sad, educated, or dull

Always liquid, flowing, changing

Seldom enduring, often forgotten.

Written words: lines in organized rhythm

Transforming thought into movement for change

Once written never to be forgotten.

## Written word

Lines; short, tall, red, or black

Drawn, stamped, itched, or sprayed


Thought; happy, sad, educated, or uninformed

Always liquid, changing seldom enduring


Written word; lines in organized rhythm

Thought once recorded never to be forgotten

## The Painter

In a small town surrounded by weeds an old house lays in disrepair
Echoes of past dreams ooze though cracked paint.
Peeling wallpaper, and warped floors cry out for relief,
From the tears of ghosts of years past.

It sings a sad ballad of neglect and pain as it slowly decays.
Yet no one hears as children throw stones at broken windows.
While passersby ignore the houses call for help
Hope fades as paint bleaches and wood decomposes.

After a time, a painter strolls by, hearing weeping he stops.
He walks over stained floors and through dilapidated rooms.
Running a calloused hand along cracked walls he feels a heartbeat.
A plan is conceived to revitalize the failing home.

With love, skilled hands restore decades of neglect.
Using a scraper. sandpaper and elbow grease
Fresh paint is skillfully brushed on mended walls and floors.

The old house renovated lives a new.

The Painter grins as he hunts for the next old house.


In a small town surrounded by empty bottles and dirty clothes a man lays in disrepair.

www.ingramcontent.com/pod-product-compliance
Lightning Source LLC
Chambersburg PA
CBHW050915160426
43194CB00011B/2411